Christopher M. Carter

# Mastering
# SAP

**A Comprehensive Guide**
**to today's SAP Software**

**Mastering SAP ... A comprehensive guide to todays SAP Software**

Copyright 2023 © Christopher M. Carter Author
SAP, SAP S/4 HANA, SAP HANA, is/are the trademark(s) or registered trademark(s) of SAP SE or its affiliates in Germany and in other countries.

**Printed by: JCHL Management**
**ISBN:** 9798393442415

**Approyo Inc.,**
W144S6311 College Ct.
Muskego, WI 53130
(414) 614-1394

# Table of Contents

# Dedication

—⟋⟋⟋—

*I hereby dedicate this book to first and foremost my family thank you for allowing me to go on this journey and for allowing me to be the "Nerd" that I am Jennifer Hannah and Lila you are my world and I appreciate everything you've allowed me to accomplish and do day in and day out.*

*I also dedicate this book to someone who I have valued and really truly believe is a genius and that is Dr. Hasso Plattner. Without your vision I would not be doing what I have been doing for over 25 years and have made supporting SAP a mission of my life.*

# About the Author

Christopher Carter is a As a Long term IT executive, he has been on the forefront of the technology revolution. He was fortunate to have been the creator of the 1st SAP cloud ever used by a SAP client in 2005, and the 1st SAP Hana Production cloud used by a true blue client.

He is currently knee deep into A.I. (Artificial Intelligence and SAP integration to support his customers thru tools and applications. He is focused on unlocking the power of your data with Approyo - the ultimate solution for SAP HANA and cloud computing with A.I.

□□2 time girl/princess Dad

Married my □ Queen

□□□Chairman/CEO of Approyo

Co-founder Impala ventures

Top □ business winner

18 time ACQ winner

2 time Inc500, 3 time Inc5000 winner

♣□♣□Cloud, A.I., Big Data, SAP/ERP executive

A three time CEO, □□□

Investor in Real estate

Investor in Classic collectibles □□

Investor in Crypto's & NFT's

Working to build new companies □🏦

Investments in people & companies

EY Entrepreneur of the year semifinalist

Global speaker of Technology & Cybersecurity

Newsmax TV contributor □

Featured in Forbes, Inc. Entrepreneur, NY Times, and many

TV/Radio SiriusXM stations/programs

Rescue □ □'s dad

A sponsor to great race drivers and their teams

Executive Producer to Radioblack band

BLESSED

# Foreword

Welcome to the world of SAP software! As businesses continue to grow and evolve, so do their technology needs. In today's fast-paced world, businesses need to manage their operations efficiently, make informed decisions, and stay ahead of the competition. This is where SAP software comes in.

SAP software is a suite of enterprise resource planning (ERP) software that helps businesses manage their operations, finances, and customer relations. With its vast range of modules and customization features, SAP software can be tailored to meet the unique needs of any business, regardless of its size or industry.

As a leading provider of ERP software, SAP has been empowering businesses around the world for more than four decades. Today, SAP software is used by businesses of all sizes and industries, from small startups to large multinational corporations.

This book is designed to provide an overview of SAP software and its various modules, along with advanced system configuration, integration, and customization. The book is intended for anyone who wants to learn about SAP software, from business owners and managers to IT professionals and SAP consultants.

The book is divided into 15 chapters, each of which covers a specific aspect of SAP software. The first chapter provides an introduction to SAP software, its history, and its features. The second chapter covers the SAP system landscape, its components, and its benefits. The third chapter covers navigating the SAP user interface, including the various screens and menus. The fourth chapter covers basic SAP system configuration, including system installation, system components, and system settings.

Chapters 5 through 10 cover the various SAP modules, including financial accounting (FI), sales and distribution (SD), materials management (MM), production planning (PP), human capital management (HCM), and business intelligence (BI). These chapters provide an in-depth overview of each module, its features, and its benefits.

Chapters 11 through 15 cover advanced system configuration, including SAP Basis administration, SAP security and authorizations, SAP Solution Manager, advanced SAP system configuration, and SAP integration and customization. These chapters provide a detailed overview of the advanced features of SAP software and how they can be used to customize and optimize the SAP system to meet the unique needs of a business.

Whether you are a business owner looking to implement SAP software, an IT professional responsible for managing the SAP system, or a consultant looking to expand your knowledge of SAP software, this book is an invaluable resource. With its comprehensive coverage of SAP software, its modules, and its advanced features, this book provides a complete overview of SAP software and its benefits.

We hope that you find this book informative and helpful in your journey to understanding and implementing SAP software.

# Introduction

— ⟋ⱮⱮ —

S AP (Systems, Applications, and Products) is an enterprise resource planning (ERP) software used by businesses of all sizes to streamline their operations, improve efficiency, and enhance productivity. With its powerful features and functionalities, SAP has become a popular choice among businesses to manage their financial, supply chain, customer relationship, and human resource management processes.

However, mastering SAP software can be a daunting task for both beginners and experienced users. This comprehensive guide aims to provide a detailed understanding of SAP software and its modules, as well as equip readers with the necessary skills to become proficient in SAP.

In this book, we will start with an introduction to SAP software, its history, and its role in enterprise management. We will then dive into the SAP system landscape and the different components that make up the SAP software. Readers will learn how to navigate the SAP user interface and perform basic system configuration tasks.

The following chapters will cover in-depth the various SAP modules, including Financial Accounting (FI), Sales and Distribution (SD), Materials Management (MM), Production Planning (PP), Human Capital Management (HCM), and Business Intelligence (BI). Each module will be explained in detail, including its functionalities and how it integrates with other modules.

We will also cover SAP Basis Administration, which includes the technical aspects of managing and maintaining an SAP system, such as database administration, system monitoring, and performance tuning. The chapter on SAP Security and Authorizations will cover how to set up user roles and permissions, ensuring that users only have access to the data they need.

Next, we will explore SAP Solution Manager, a tool used to manage and monitor SAP systems. We will discuss its functionalities, including system monitoring, incident management, and change request management.

In the final chapters, we will cover advanced SAP system configuration, including system customization and enhancement. We will also cover SAP integration with other software and systems, including third-party software and cloud services.

By the end of this book, readers will have a thorough understanding of SAP software and its modules, as well as the necessary skills to become proficient in SAP. Whether you are a beginner or an experienced SAP user, this book is an essential guide to mastering SAP software.

# 1

—ᴡᴡ—

## Introduction To Sap Software

SAP software is a suite of enterprise management applications used by businesses of all sizes to streamline their operations and improve efficiency. In this chapter, we will provide an overview of SAP software, its history, and its role in enterprise management.

SAP was founded in 1972 in Germany by five former IBM engineers. The company's first product was a financial accounting software called R/1. Since then, SAP has grown to become one of the largest software companies in the world, with over 200 million users and more than 440,000 customers in 180 countries.

SAP software is designed to integrate all aspects of a business's operations, including financial management, supply chain management, customer relationship management, and human resource management. It provides a centralized system for managing business processes, which can help businesses reduce costs, improve efficiency, and enhance

SAP (Systems, Applications, and Products) is an enterprise resource planning (ERP) software that is used by businesses of all sizes to manage their operations, improve efficiency, and enhance productivity. With its powerful features and functionalities, SAP has become a popular choice among businesses to manage their financial, supply chain, customer relationship, and human resource management processes.

In this chapter, we will provide an overview of SAP software, its history, and its role in enterprise management.

## History of SAP Software:

SAP was founded in 1972 in Germany by five former IBM engineers: Dietmar Hopp, Hasso Plattner, Claus Wellenreuther, Klaus Tschira, and Werner Brandt. The company's first product was a financial accounting software called R/1, which was released in 1973. R/1 was a client-server architecture software that ran on IBM mainframe computers.

In the 1980s, SAP released its second-generation product, R/2, which was a mainframe-based software used for managing complex business processes. In the 1990s, SAP shifted its focus to client-server architecture and released its third-generation product, R/3. R/3 was a client-server architecture software that ran on UNIX and Windows operating systems.

Since then, SAP has continued to innovate and release new products and services, including SAP HANA (High-Performance Analytic Appliance), a database management system that combines database, data processing, and application platform capabilities.

## Overview of SAP Software:

SAP software is a suite of enterprise management applications that are designed to integrate all aspects of a business's operations. It provides a centralized system for managing business processes, which can help businesses reduce costs, improve efficiency, and enhance productivity.

SAP software is modular in design, which means that businesses can choose the modules they need based on their specific requirements. Some of the key modules of SAP software include:

1. **Financial Accounting (FI) Module:** The FI module of SAP software is used for managing financial transactions, including general ledger, accounts payable, accounts receivable, and asset accounting.

2. **Sales and Distribution (SD) Module:** The SD module of SAP software is used for managing sales and distribution processes, including sales orders, deliveries, and invoicing.

3. **Materials Management (MM) Module:** The MM module of SAP software is used for managing procurement processes, including purchasing, inventory management, and material valuation.

4. **Production Planning (PP) Module:** The PP module of SAP software is used for managing production processes, including production planning, material requirements planning, and capacity planning.

5. **Human Capital Management (HCM) Module:** The HCM module of SAP software is used for managing human resource processes, including employee data management, payroll, and benefits administration.

6. **Business Intelligence (BI) Module:** The BI module of SAP software is used for reporting and analysis, including data warehousing, data mining, and data visualization.

## Role of SAP Software in Enterprise Management:

SAP software plays a crucial role in enterprise management by providing a centralized system for managing business processes. It enables businesses to integrate and streamline their operations, which can help them reduce costs, improve efficiency, and enhance productivity.

Some of the key benefits of using SAP software include:

1. **Improved visibility:** SAP software provides real-time visibility into business operations, which can help businesses make informed decisions based on accurate data.

2. **Streamlined processes:** SAP software enables businesses to automate and streamline their processes, which can help them save time and reduce errors.

3. **Enhanced productivity:** SAP software provides employees with the tools and information they need to work more efficiently, which can help businesses enhance productivity.

4. **Better customer service:** SAP software enables businesses to manage customer relationships more effectively.

# 2

—⁓—

# Understanding the SAP System Landscape

The SAP system landscape is the technical infrastructure that supports the operation of SAP software. The SAP system landscape consists of various components, including hardware, software, and network infrastructure.

In this chapter, we will provide an overview of the SAP system landscape, its components, and their roles in supporting the operation of SAP software.

## SAP System Landscape Components:

The SAP system landscape consists of the following components:

1. **Application Server:** The application server is the core component of the SAP system landscape. It runs the SAP software and provides the computing resources necessary to execute the software.

2. **Database Server:** The database server is responsible for storing and managing the data used by SAP software. It is typically a relational database management system (RDBMS), such as Oracle, Microsoft SQL Server, or SAP HANA.

3. **Presentation Server:** The presentation server is the component that runs the user interface for SAP software. It is typically a Windows or Linux-based computer.

4. **Client:** The client is the component that connects to the application server and runs the SAP software. The client can be a desktop computer or a mobile device.

5. **Network Infrastructure:** The network infrastructure provides the connectivity necessary for the different components of the SAP system landscape to communicate with each other. It includes routers, switches, firewalls, and other networking devices.

## SAP System Landscape Types:

The SAP system landscape can be configured in various ways depending on the needs of the business. The most common SAP system landscape types include:

1. **Development Landscape:** The development landscape is used for developing and testing new SAP software applications. It typically consists of a single server running the SAP software, a database server, and a presentation server.

2. **Quality Assurance Landscape:** The quality assurance landscape is used for testing the SAP software before it is deployed to production. It typically consists of a single server running the SAP software, a database server, and a presentation server.

3. **Production Landscape:** The production landscape is the live environment where the SAP software is used to manage business operations. It typically consists of multiple servers running the SAP software, a database server, and a presentation server.

4. **Disaster Recovery Landscape:** The disaster recovery landscape is used for restoring the SAP system in the event of a disaster, such as a hardware failure or natural disaster. It typically consists of a replica of the production landscape running in a separate location.

## SAP System Landscape Architecture:

The SAP system landscape architecture is the way in which the various components of the SAP system landscape are organized and connected. There are two main SAP system landscape architectures:

1. **Single System Landscape:** In a single system landscape architecture, all components of the SAP system landscape are

installed on a single server. This architecture is typically used for small businesses with limited IT resources.

2. **Distributed System Landscape:** In a distributed system landscape architecture, the different components of the SAP system landscape are distributed across multiple servers. This architecture is typically used for larger businesses with more complex IT requirements.

## SAP System Landscape Considerations:

When designing the SAP system landscape, there are several considerations that must be taken into account. These considerations include:

1. **Scalability:** The SAP system landscape must be able to scale to accommodate the growth of the business.

2. **Availability:** The SAP system landscape must be highly available to ensure that the business operations can continue even in the event of a hardware or software failure.

3. **Security:** The SAP system landscape must be secure to prevent unauthorized access to sensitive business data.

4. **Performance:** The SAP system landscape must be optimized for performance to ensure that the SAP software can execute efficiently.

## Conclusion:

Understanding the SAP system landscape is critical for businesses that are planning to implement the SAP system. By understanding the

SAP system architecture, the various components of the SAP system landscape, and the benefits of using the SAP system, businesses can make informed decisions about the configuration and customization of the SAP system landscape.

The SAP system landscape provides various benefits to businesses, including improved business efficiency, better decision-making, enhanced productivity, and reduced costs. By using the SAP system, businesses can streamline their business processes, gain insights into their operations, improve productivity, and reduce costs.

By customizing the SAP system landscape to meet the unique needs of a business, businesses can configure the SAP system to support specific business processes and improve efficiency. Customization features like system architecture, system components, and system configuration enable businesses to tailor the SAP system to their specific needs.

Overall, understanding the SAP system landscape is critical for businesses that are planning to implement the SAP system. By using the SAP system landscape effectively, businesses can improve their operations and achieve their business goals.

# 3

—ᴡ—

## Navigating the SAP User Interface

The SAP user interface (UI) is the visual interface that allows users to interact with SAP software.

The SAP UI is designed to be user-friendly and intuitive, but it can be complex and overwhelming for new users. In this chapter, we will provide an overview of the SAP user interface and how to navigate it.

## SAP User Interface Components:

The SAP user interface consists of various components that work together to provide a comprehensive and interactive user experience. Some of the key SAP UI components include:

1. **Menu Bar:** The menu bar is located at the top of the SAP screen and provides access to various SAP functions and applications.

2. **Toolbar:** The toolbar is located directly below the menu bar and contains buttons for frequently used SAP functions.

3. **Navigation Pane:** The navigation pane is located on the left side of the SAP screen and provides access to different areas of the SAP software.

4. **Work Area:** The work area is the main area of the SAP screen and displays the content of the selected SAP function or application.

5. **Status Bar:** The status bar is located at the bottom of the SAP screen and displays information about the current SAP function or application.

## Navigating the SAP User Interface:

Navigating the SAP user interface can be challenging for new users. However, with practice, it can become easier to navigate and use. Here are some tips to help navigate the SAP user interface:

1. **Use the Menu Bar:** The menu bar is a useful tool for navigating the SAP user interface. It provides access to various SAP functions and applications, and it can be

customized to display only the functions that are relevant to the user.

2. **Use the Navigation Pane:** The navigation pane is a useful tool for navigating different areas of the SAP software. It provides access to different functions and applications within the SAP software, and it can be customized to display only the functions that are relevant to the user.

3. **Use the Toolbar:** The toolbar is a useful tool for accessing frequently used SAP functions. It contains buttons for functions such as saving, printing, and navigating to previous screens.

4. **Use Shortcuts:** SAP provides various shortcuts that can help users navigate the SAP user interface more efficiently. For example, the F4 key can be used to display a list of values for a particular field, and the F1 key can be used to access the SAP help system.

5. **Customize the User Interface:** The SAP user interface can be customized to suit the user's preferences. For example, the font size and color can be changed, and the menu bar and navigation pane can be customized to display only the functions that are relevant to the user.

## Conclusion:

The SAP user interface is a powerful tool for managing business operations.

While it can be complex and overwhelming for new users, with practice and familiarity, it can become easier to navigate and use. By using the menu bar, navigation pane, toolbar, shortcuts, and customization features, users can efficiently navigate the SAP user interface and manage their business operations effectively.

# 4

—m—

## Basic SAP System Configuration

System configuration is an essential part of setting up and using SAP software. SAP system configuration involves setting up various system parameters, such as user roles, authorization profiles, and company codes, to ensure that the SAP software is configured to meet the business requirements.

In this chapter, we will provide an overview of the basic SAP system configuration and the various system parameters that need to be configured.

## Basic SAP System Configuration Parameters:

The basic SAP system configuration parameters that need to be configured include:

1. **Client:** The client is a logical unit in the SAP system that represents a business entity or group of business entities. Each client has its own set of data, such as master data and transactional data. The SAP system can have multiple clients, and each client can have its own configuration settings.

2. **Company Code:** The company code represents a legal entity within a client. Each company code has its own set of accounting data, such as chart of accounts and fiscal year variant. The company code is used to generate financial statements and reports.

3. **User Roles:** User roles define the functions and activities that a user can perform within the SAP system. User roles are assigned to users based on their job responsibilities.

4. **Authorization Profiles:** Authorization profiles define the level of access that a user has to different functions and activities within the SAP system. Authorization profiles are assigned to users based on their user roles.

5. **Currency:** The currency is the unit of measure for financial transactions in the SAP system. The currency is defined at the client and company code levels.

6. **Fiscal Year Variant:** The fiscal year variant defines the start and end dates of the fiscal year for a company code. The fiscal

year variant is used to generate financial statements and reports.

7. **Posting Period Variant:** The posting period variant defines the periods for posting accounting transactions in the SAP system. The posting period variant is used to ensure that transactions are posted in the correct accounting period.

8. **Chart of Accounts:** The chart of accounts is a list of all the accounts that are used in the SAP system for recording financial transactions. The chart of accounts is defined at the client level and is used by all company codes within the client.

9. **Tax Codes:** Tax codes are used to define the tax rates and rules for different types of transactions within the SAP system. Tax codes are defined at the client and company code levels.

10. **Output Devices:** Output devices are used to generate and print reports and documents within the SAP system. Output devices can be printers or electronic devices, such as email or fax.

## SAP System Configuration Process:

The SAP system configuration process involves the following steps:

1. **Planning:** The planning phase involves identifying the business requirements and determining the system configuration parameters that need to be set up.

2. **Configuration:** The configuration phase involves setting up the system configuration parameters in the SAP system.

3. **Testing:** The testing phase involves testing the configured system parameters to ensure that they are working correctly and meet the business requirements.

4. **Documentation:** The documentation phase involves documenting the system configuration parameters and the testing results.

5. **Maintenance:** The maintenance phase involves maintaining the system configuration parameters and updating them as necessary to meet changing business requirements.

## Best Practices for SAP System Configuration:

Here are some best practices for SAP system configuration:

1. Define a clear system configuration plan and adhere to it throughout the configuration process.

2. Use the SAP standard configuration whenever possible to ensure compatibility and easy maintenance.

3. Document all system configuration settings and testing results.

4. Test the system configuration thoroughly to ensure that it meets the business requirements.

5. Perform regular system configuration maintenance to ensure that the SAP software is always configured to meet the changing business requirements.

## Conclusion:

In this chapter, we provided an overview of the basic configuration of the SAP system, its components, and its benefits. We covered the SAP system installation process, the various components of the SAP system, and the benefits of basic system configuration.

We discussed how the SAP system can be installed using the SAPinst tool, which automates the installation process and ensures that the SAP system is configured correctly. We also discussed the various components of the SAP system, including the SAP application server, the database server, the client, and the presentation server.

We also discussed the benefits of basic system configuration, including improved system performance, enhanced security, and improved system stability. By configuring the SAP system correctly, businesses can improve system performance, reduce system downtime, and prevent security breaches.

Finally, we discussed how the SAP system can be customized to meet the unique needs of a business. By using the customization features of the SAP system, businesses can configure the SAP system to support specific business processes and improve efficiency.

Basic SAP system configuration is critical for businesses that are planning to implement the SAP system. By understanding the SAP system installation process, the various components of the SAP system, and the benefits of basic system configuration, businesses can make informed decisions about the configuration and customization of the SAP system.

The SAP system installation process can be automated using the SAPinst tool, which ensures that the SAP system is configured correctly and reduces the risk of errors. The various components of the SAP system, including the SAP application server, the database server, the client, and the presentation server, must be configured correctly to ensure that the SAP system functions properly.

Basic system configuration provides various benefits to businesses, including improved system performance, enhanced security, and improved system stability. By configuring the SAP system correctly, businesses can improve system performance, reduce system downtime, and prevent security breaches.

By customizing the SAP system to meet the unique needs of a business, businesses can configure the SAP system to support specific business processes and improve efficiency. Customization features like system architecture, system components, and system configuration enable businesses to tailor the SAP system to their specific needs.

Overall, basic SAP system configuration is critical for businesses that are planning to implement the SAP system. By configuring the SAP system correctly and customizing it to meet the unique needs of a business, businesses can improve their operations and achieve their business goals.

# 5

---∽m∽---

## SAP Financial Accounting (FI) Module

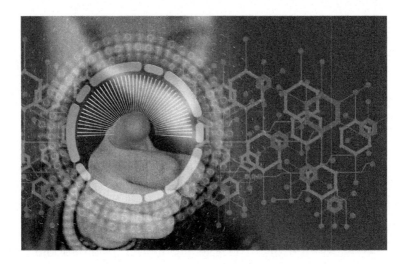

The SAP Financial Accounting (FI) module is one of the core modules of SAP software. The SAP FI module is designed to manage the financial transactions and accounting processes of a business. In this chapter, we will provide an overview of the SAP FI module, its features, and its benefits.

## Features of SAP Financial Accounting (FI) Module:

The SAP FI module provides various features to help manage financial transactions and accounting processes. Some of the key features of the SAP FI module include:

1. **General Ledger Accounting:** The general ledger accounting feature of the SAP FI module is used to manage the financial transactions of a business. It provides a complete view of the financial transactions and the financial position of the business.

2. **Accounts Receivable:** The accounts receivable feature of the SAP FI module is used to manage the customer invoices and receipts. It tracks the outstanding customer balances and generates reports on customer account balances.

3. **Accounts Payable:** The accounts payable feature of the SAP FI module is used to manage the vendor invoices and payments. It tracks the outstanding vendor balances and generates reports on vendor account balances.

4. **Asset Accounting:** The asset accounting feature of the SAP FI module is used to manage the fixed assets of a business. It tracks the acquisition, depreciation, and disposal of fixed assets and generates reports on the fixed asset balances.

5. **Bank Accounting:** The bank accounting feature of the SAP FI module is used to manage the bank transactions of a business. It tracks the bank transactions and generates reports on the bank balances.

## Benefits of SAP Financial Accounting (FI) Module:

The SAP FI module provides various benefits to a business. Some of the key benefits of the SAP FI module include:

1. **Improved Financial Management:** The SAP FI module provides a complete view of the financial transactions and the financial position of the business. It enables the business to manage its finances more effectively and make informed financial decisions.

2. **Increased Efficiency:** The SAP FI module automates many financial transactions and accounting processes, which increases efficiency and reduces manual errors.

3. **Improved Control:** The SAP FI module provides greater control over financial transactions and accounting processes. It enables the business to enforce financial policies and procedures and ensure compliance with regulatory requirements.

4. **Greater Visibility:** The SAP FI module provides greater visibility into financial transactions and accounting processes. It enables the business to generate reports on financial performance and make informed decisions.

5. **Integration with Other Modules:** The SAP FI module integrates with other SAP modules, such as SAP Controlling (CO)

## Conclusion:

The SAP Financial Accounting (FI) module is a core module of the SAP system that is used to manage financial accounting data within an organization.

By using the general ledger, accounts receivable, accounts payable, asset accounting, and bank accounting features of the SAP FI module, businesses can efficiently manage their financial accounting data and improve financial control, reporting, accounts receivable and accounts payable management, asset accounting, and bank accounting.

The SAP FI module provides various benefits, such as improved financial control, improved financial reporting, efficient accounts receivable and accounts payable management, accurate asset accounting, and efficient bank accounting.

# 6

---m---

## SAP Sales and Distribution (SD) Module

The SAP Sales and Distribution (SD) module is one of the core modules of SAP software. The SAP SD module is designed to manage the sales and distribution processes of a business. In this chapter, we will provide an overview of the SAP SD module, its features, and its benefits.

## Features of SAP Sales and Distribution (SD) Module:

The SAP SD module provides various features to help manage the sales and distribution processes of a business. Some of the key features of the SAP SD module include:

1. **Sales Order Management:** The sales order management feature of the SAP SD module is used to manage the sales order process. It enables the business to create, process, and track sales orders, from quotation to delivery.

2. **Pricing and Discounts:** The pricing and discounts feature of the SAP SD module is used to manage the pricing and discount policies of a business. It enables the business to set up different pricing policies and discounts for different customers.

3. **Billing and Invoicing:** The billing and invoicing feature of the SAP SD module is used to manage the billing and invoicing processes of a business. It enables the business to generate invoices, credit notes, and debit notes, and track the payment status of invoices.

4. **Shipping and Transportation:** The shipping and transportation feature of the SAP SD module is used to manage the shipping and transportation processes of a business. It enables the business to create and track shipments, and generate shipping and transportation documents.

5. **Credit Management:** The credit management feature of the SAP SD module is used to manage the credit limits and credit control processes of a business. It enables the business to set

up credit limits for customers and control the credit usage of customers.

## Benefits of SAP Sales and Distribution (SD) Module:

The SAP SD module provides various benefits to a business. Some of the key benefits of the SAP SD module include:

1. **Improved Sales Management:** The SAP SD module provides a complete view of the sales process, from quotation to delivery. It enables the business to manage its sales more effectively and make informed sales decisions.

2. **Increased Efficiency:** The SAP SD module automates many sales and distribution processes, which increases efficiency and reduces manual errors.

3. **Improved Customer Satisfaction:** The SAP SD module provides a better customer experience by enabling the business to provide accurate and timely sales information to customers.

4. **Greater Visibility:** The SAP SD module provides greater visibility into the sales and distribution processes. It enables the business to generate reports on sales performance and make informed decisions.

5. **Integration with Other Modules:** The SAP SD module integrates with other SAP modules, such as SAP Financial Accounting (FI) and SAP Controlling (CO), to provide a complete view of the business processes.

## Conclusion:

The SAP Sales and Distribution (SD) module is a powerful tool for managing the sales and distribution processes of a business.

By using the sales order management, pricing and discounts, billing and invoicing, shipping and transportation, and credit management features of the SAP SD module, businesses can efficiently manage their sales operations and improve their customer satisfaction.

The SAP SD module provides various benefits, such as improved sales management, increased efficiency, improved customer satisfaction, greater visibility, and integration with other SAP modules.

# 7

—⟋ɱↃ—

## SAP Materials Management (MM) Module

The SAP Materials Management (MM) module is one of the core modules of SAP software. The SAP MM module is designed to manage the materials and inventory processes of a business. In this chapter, we will provide an overview of the SAP MM module, its features, and its benefits.

### Features of SAP Materials Management (MM) Module:

The SAP MM module provides various features to help manage the materials and inventory processes of a business. Some of the key features of the SAP MM module include:

1. **Procurement:** The procurement feature of the SAP MM module is used to manage the procurement process, from requisition to purchase order. It enables the business to create and manage purchase orders, and track the status of procurement activities.

2. **Inventory Management:** The inventory management feature of the SAP MM module is used to manage the inventory of a business. It enables the business to track inventory levels, manage inventory movements, and generate inventory reports.

3. **Material Master:** The material master feature of the SAP MM module is used to manage the material master data. It enables the business to create and maintain the material master data, such as material codes, descriptions, and attributes.

4. **Invoice Verification:** The invoice verification feature of the SAP MM module is used to manage the invoice verification process. It enables the business to verify invoices against purchase orders and goods receipts, and reconcile any discrepancies.

5. **Vendor Management:** The vendor management feature of the SAP MM module is used to manage the vendor master data. It enables the business to create and maintain the vendor master data, such as vendor codes, names, and addresses.

## Benefits of SAP Materials Management (MM) Module:

The SAP MM module provides various benefits to a business. Some of the key benefits of the SAP MM module include:

1.  **Improved Materials Management:** The SAP MM module provides a complete view of the materials and inventory processes of a business. It enables the business to manage its materials and inventory more effectively and make informed materials management decisions.

2.  **Increased Efficiency:** The SAP MM module automates many materials and inventory processes, which increases efficiency and reduces manual errors.

3.  **Improved Vendor Management:** The SAP MM module provides a better vendor management experience by enabling the business to manage its vendors more effectively and make informed vendor management decisions.

4.  **Greater Visibility:** The SAP MM module provides greater visibility into the materials and inventory processes. It enables the business to generate reports on materials and inventory performance and make informed decisions.

5.  **Integration with Other Modules:** The SAP MM module integrates with other SAP modules, such as SAP Financial Accounting (FI) and SAP Sales and Distribution (SD), to provide a complete view of the business processes.

## Conclusion:

The SAP Materials Management (MM) module is a powerful tool for managing the materials and inventory processes of a business.

By using the procurement, inventory management, material master, invoice verification, and vendor management features of the SAP

MM module, businesses can efficiently manage their materials and inventory operations and improve their materials management decisions.

The SAP MM module provides various benefits, such as improved materials management, increased efficiency, improved vendor management, greater visibility, and integration with other SAP modules.

# 8

—ɯ—

## SAP Production Planning (PP) Module

The SAP Production Planning (PP) module is one of the core modules of SAP software. The SAP PP module is designed to manage the production planning and control processes of a business. In this chapter, we will provide an overview of the SAP PP module, its features, and its benefits.

## Features of SAP Production Planning (PP) Module:

The SAP PP module provides various features to help manage the production planning and control processes of a business. Some of the key features of the SAP PP module include:

1. **Master Production Scheduling:** The master production scheduling feature of the SAP PP module is used to manage the production planning process. It enables the business to create and manage the master production schedule, which defines the production plan for the business.

2. **Capacity Planning:** The capacity planning feature of the SAP PP module is used to manage the capacity requirements of the production plan. It enables the business to determine the resources required to produce the products and optimize the production plan accordingly.

3. **Bill of Materials:** The bill of materials feature of the SAP PP module is used to manage the product structure and component information. It enables the business to create and maintain the bill of materials data, such as material codes, descriptions, and quantities.

4. **Shop Floor Control:** The shop floor control feature of the SAP PP module is used to manage the production process on the shop floor. It enables the business to track the progress of production orders, and manage the shop floor activities, such as material movements and quality inspections.

5. **Material Requirements Planning:** The material requirements planning feature of the SAP PP module is used to manage the

material requirements for production. It enables the business to determine the materials required for production and plan the procurement accordingly.

## Benefits of SAP Production Planning (PP) Module:

The SAP PP module provides various benefits to a business. Some of the key benefits of the SAP PP module include:

1. **Improved Production Planning:** The SAP PP module provides a complete view of the production planning process. It enables the business to manage its production planning more effectively and make informed production planning decisions.

2. **Increased Efficiency:** The SAP PP module automates many production planning processes, which increases efficiency and reduces manual errors.

3. **Improved Resource Utilization:** The SAP PP module provides a better resource utilization experience by enabling the business to optimize the production plan based on the available resources.

4. **Greater Visibility:** The SAP PP module provides greater visibility into the production planning and control processes. It enables the business to generate reports on production performance and make informed decisions.

5. **Integration with Other Modules:** The SAP PP module integrates with other SAP modules, such as SAP Materials Management (MM) and SAP Sales and Distribution (SD), to provide a complete view of the business processes.

## Conclusion:

The SAP Production Planning (PP) module is a powerful tool for managing the production planning and control processes of a business.

By using the master production scheduling, capacity planning, bill of materials, shop floor control, and material requirements planning features of the SAP PP module, businesses can efficiently manage their production operations and improve their production planning decisions.

The SAP PP module provides various benefits, such as improved production planning, increased efficiency, improved resource utilization, greater visibility, and integration with other SAP modules.

# 9

—ɯ—

## SAP Human Capital Management (HCM) Module

The SAP Human Capital Management (HCM) module is one of the core modules of SAP software. The SAP HCM module is designed to manage the human resources (HR) processes of a business. In this chapter, we will provide an overview of the SAP HCM module, its features, and its benefits.

## Features of SAP Human Capital Management (HCM) Module:

The SAP HCM module provides various features to help manage the human resources (HR) processes of a business. Some of the key features of the SAP HCM module include:

1.  Organizational Management: The organizational management feature of the SAP HCM module is used to manage the organizational structure of a business. It enables the business to create and maintain the organizational hierarchy, positions, and job descriptions.

2.  Personnel Administration: The personnel administration feature of the SAP HCM module is used to manage the employee data of a business. It enables the business to create and maintain employee master data, such as personal data, employment data, and organizational data.

3.  Time and Attendance Management: The time and attendance management feature of the SAP HCM module is used to manage the time and attendance data of employees. It enables the business to track employee working hours, absence, and leave data.

4.  Payroll Management: The payroll management feature of the SAP HCM module is used to manage the payroll process of a business. It enables the business to calculate and process employee salaries, taxes, and other payroll-related data.

5.  Talent Management: The talent management feature of the SAP HCM module is used to manage the talent development

and succession planning processes of a business. It enables the business to identify and develop the talent of its employees, and plan for their career growth within the organization.

## Benefits of SAP Human Capital Management (HCM) Module:

The SAP HCM module provides various benefits to a business. Some of the key benefits of the SAP HCM module include:

1. **Improved HR Management:** The SAP HCM module provides a complete view of the HR processes of a business. It enables the business to manage its HR more effectively and make informed HR decisions.

2. **Increased Efficiency:** The SAP HCM module automates many HR processes, which increases efficiency and reduces manual errors.

3. **Improved Employee Engagement:** The SAP HCM module provides a better employee experience by enabling the business to manage the employee data and development more effectively.

4. **Greater Visibility:** The SAP HCM module provides greater visibility into the HR processes. It enables the business to generate reports on HR performance and make informed decisions.

5. **Integration with Other Modules:** The SAP HCM module integrates with other SAP modules, such as SAP Financial

Accounting (FI) and SAP Sales and Distribution (SD), to provide a complete view of the business processes.

## Conclusion:

The SAP Human Capital Management (HCM) module is a powerful tool for managing the human resources (HR) processes of a business.

By using the organizational management, personnel administration, time and attendance management, payroll management, and talent management features of the SAP HCM module, businesses can efficiently manage their HR operations and improve their HR decisions.

The SAP HCM module provides various benefits, such as improved HR management, increased efficiency, improved employee engagement, greater visibility, and integration with other SAP modules.

# 10

## SAP Business Intelligence (BI) Module

The SAP Business Intelligence (BI) module is one of the core modules of SAP software. The SAP BI module is designed to manage the business intelligence and analytics processes of a business. In this chapter, we will provide an overview of the SAP BI module, its features, and its benefits.

## Features of SAP Business Intelligence (BI) Module:

The SAP BI module provides various features to help manage the business intelligence and analytics processes of a business. Some of the key features of the SAP BI module include:

1.  **Reporting:** The reporting feature of the SAP BI module is used to generate reports on various business metrics, such as sales, revenue, and profit. It enables the business to analyze the data and make informed decisions.

2.  **Data Visualization:** The data visualization feature of the SAP BI module is used to visualize the data in various formats, such as charts, graphs, and tables. It enables the business to interpret the data more effectively and make informed decisions.

3.  **Data Mining:** The data mining feature of the SAP BI module is used to identify patterns and trends in the data. It enables the business to analyze the data and make informed decisions.

4.  **Data Warehousing:** The data warehousing feature of the SAP BI module is used to store and manage large volumes of data. It enables the business to analyze the data more effectively and make informed decisions.

5.  **Business Planning and Consolidation:** The business planning and consolidation feature of the SAP BI module is used to manage the budgeting and forecasting processes of a business. It enables the business to plan and forecast its future financial performance.

## Benefits of SAP Business Intelligence (BI) Module:

The SAP BI module provides various benefits to a business. Some of the key benefits of the SAP BI module include:

1. **Improved Decision Making:** The SAP BI module provides a complete view of the business data. It enables the business to analyze the data and make informed decisions.

2. **Increased Efficiency:** The SAP BI module automates many business intelligence and analytics processes, which increases efficiency and reduces manual errors.

3. **Improved Data Interpretation:** The SAP BI module provides a better data interpretation experience by enabling the business to visualize the data in various formats.

4. **Greater Visibility:** The SAP BI module provides greater visibility into the business data. It enables the business to generate reports on business performance and make informed decisions.

5. **Integration with Other Modules:** The SAP BI module integrates with other SAP modules, such as SAP Sales and Distribution (SD) and SAP Materials Management (MM), to provide a complete view of the business processes.

## Conclusion:

The SAP Business Intelligence (BI) module is a powerful tool for managing the business intelligence and analytics processes of a business.

By using the reporting, data visualization, data mining, data warehousing, and business planning and consolidation features of the SAP BI module, businesses can efficiently manage their business data and improve their decision-making processes.

The SAP BI module provides various benefits, such as improved decision-making, increased efficiency, improved data interpretation, greater visibility, and integration with other SAP modules.

# 11

—ᴍ—

## SAP Basis Administration

S AP Basis Administration is the foundation of SAP software. It is responsible for managing the technical infrastructure of the SAP system, which includes the operating system, database, and SAP software components. In this chapter, we will provide an overview of SAP Basis Administration, its features, and its benefits.

## Features of SAP Basis Administration:

SAP Basis Administration provides various features to help manage the technical infrastructure of the SAP system. Some of the key features of SAP Basis Administration include:

1. **System Monitoring:** The system monitoring feature of SAP Basis Administration is used to monitor the performance and health of the SAP system. It enables the business to identify and resolve issues before they impact the system.

2. **User and Authorization Management:** The user and authorization management feature of SAP Basis Administration is used to manage the user accounts and authorizations in the SAP system. It enables the business to control access to the SAP system and protect sensitive data.

3. **Backup and Recovery:** The backup and recovery feature of SAP Basis Administration is used to create backups of the SAP system and restore them in the event of a system failure. It enables the business to minimize data loss and reduce system downtime.

4. **System Upgrades and Patching:** The system upgrades and patching feature of SAP Basis Administration is used to upgrade the SAP system and apply patches to fix known issues. It enables the business to keep the SAP system up to date and secure.

5. **System Performance Optimization:** The system performance optimization feature of SAP Basis

Administration is used to optimize the performance of the SAP system. It enables the business to improve system response times and reduce system downtime.

## Benefits of SAP Basis Administration:

SAP Basis Administration provides various benefits to a business. Some of the key benefits of SAP Basis Administration include:

1. **Improved System Stability:** SAP Basis Administration ensures that the SAP system is stable and performing optimally. It enables the business to avoid system downtime and improve system availability.

2. **Increased Security:** SAP Basis Administration ensures that the SAP system is secure and protected from unauthorized access. It enables the business to protect sensitive data and comply with regulatory requirements.

3. **Efficient System Maintenance:** SAP Basis Administration automates many system maintenance processes, which increases efficiency and reduces manual errors.

4. **Faster Issue Resolution:** SAP Basis Administration enables the business to identify and resolve issues quickly, which reduces system downtime and improves system availability.

5. **Integration with Other SAP Modules:** SAP Basis Administration integrates with other SAP modules, such as SAP Financial Accounting (FI) and SAP Sales and Distribution (SD), to provide a complete view of the business processes.

## Conclusion:

SAP Basis Administration is a critical component of the SAP system.

By using the system monitoring, user and authorization management, backup and recovery, system upgrades and patching, and system performance optimization features of SAP Basis Administration, businesses can efficiently manage the technical infrastructure of the SAP system and ensure system stability and security.

SAP Basis Administration provides various benefits, such as improved system stability, increased security, efficient system maintenance, faster issue resolution, and integration with other SAP modules.

# 12

## SAP Security and Authorizations

S AP Security and Authorizations is a critical component of the SAP system. It is responsible for managing the access control and security of the SAP system. In this chapter, we will provide an overview of SAP Security and Authorizations, its features, and its benefits.

## Features of SAP Security and Authorizations:

SAP Security and Authorizations provides various features to help manage the access control and security of the SAP system. Some of the key features of SAP Security and Authorizations include:

1. **User and Role Management:** The user and role management feature of SAP Security and Authorizations is used to manage user accounts and roles in the SAP system. It enables the business to control access to the SAP system and protect sensitive data.

2. **Authorization Concept:** The authorization concept feature of SAP Security and Authorizations is used to define and manage authorization objects and authorization profiles in the SAP system. It enables the business to control access to specific SAP transactions and functions.

3. **Security Audit:** The security audit feature of SAP Security and Authorizations is used to monitor and audit the security of the SAP system. It enables the business to identify and resolve security issues before they impact the system.

4. **Encryption and Decryption:** The encryption and decryption feature of SAP Security and Authorizations is used to encrypt and decrypt sensitive data in the SAP system. It enables the business to protect sensitive data and comply with regulatory requirements.

5. **Single Sign-On:** The single sign-on feature of SAP Security and Authorizations is used to enable users to access the SAP

system using a single set of credentials. It enables the business to simplify the user login process and improve user experience.

## Benefits of SAP Security and Authorizations:

SAP Security and Authorizations provides various benefits to a business. Some of the key benefits of SAP Security and Authorizations include:

1.  **Improved System Security:** SAP Security and Authorizations ensures that the SAP system is secure and protected from unauthorized access. It enables the business to protect sensitive data and comply with regulatory requirements.

2.  **Efficient Access Control:** SAP Security and Authorizations enables the business to efficiently manage access control in the SAP system. It enables the business to control access to specific SAP transactions and functions.

3.  **Effective Security Auditing:** SAP Security and Authorizations enables the business to effectively monitor and audit the security of the SAP system. It enables the business to identify and resolve security issues before they impact the system.

4.  **Simplified User Management:** SAP Security and Authorizations enables the business to simplify user management in the SAP system. It enables the business to manage user accounts and roles more efficiently.

5. **Integration with Other SAP Modules:** SAP Security and Authorizations integrates with other SAP modules, such as SAP Financial Accounting (FI) and SAP Sales and Distribution (SD), to provide a complete view of the business processes.

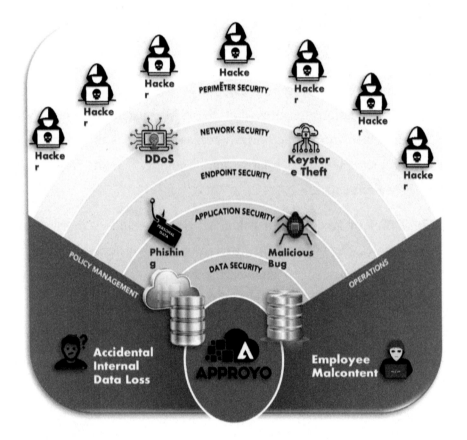

## Conclusion:

SAP Security and Authorizations is a critical component of the SAP system.

By using the user and role management, authorization concept, security audit, encryption and decryption, and single sign-on features of SAP Security and Authorizations, businesses can efficiently manage the access control and security of the SAP system and protect sensitive data.

SAP Security and Authorizations provides various benefits, such as improved system security, efficient access control, effective security auditing, simplified user management, and integration with other SAP modules.

# 13

—m—

## SAP Solution Manager

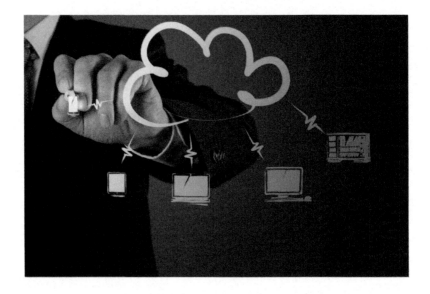

S AP Solution Manager is a centralized application management and support solution for SAP software.

It provides various features to help manage the entire lifecycle of an SAP system, from implementation to maintenance. In this chapter, we will provide an overview of SAP Solution Manager, its features, and its benefits.

## Features of SAP Solution Manager:

SAP Solution Manager provides various features to help manage the entire lifecycle of an SAP system. Some of the key features of SAP Solution Manager include:

1. **System Monitoring:** The system monitoring feature of SAP Solution Manager is used to monitor the performance and health of the SAP system. It enables the business to identify and resolve issues before they impact the system.

2. **Change Request Management:** The change request management feature of SAP Solution Manager is used to manage the change requests in the SAP system. It enables the business to control changes to the SAP system and minimize system downtime.

3. **Test Management:** The test management feature of SAP Solution Manager is used to manage the testing processes in the SAP system. It enables the business to ensure that changes to the SAP system do not impact the business processes.

4. **Incident Management:** The incident management feature of SAP Solution Manager is used to manage the incidents in the SAP system. It enables the business to identify and resolve issues in the SAP system.

5. **Technical Monitoring:** The technical monitoring feature of SAP Solution Manager is used to monitor the technical infrastructure of the SAP system, such as the operating system and database. It enables the business to identify and resolve technical issues before they impact the SAP system.

## Benefits of SAP Solution Manager:

SAP Solution Manager provides various benefits to a business. Some of the key benefits of SAP Solution Manager include:

1. **Improved System Stability:** SAP Solution Manager ensures that the SAP system is stable and performing optimally. It enables the business to avoid system downtime and improve system availability.

2. **Increased Efficiency:** SAP Solution Manager automates many SAP management processes, which increases efficiency and reduces manual errors.

3. **Faster Issue Resolution:** SAP Solution Manager enables the business to identify and resolve issues quickly, which reduces system downtime and improves system availability.

4. **Simplified System Management:** SAP Solution Manager provides a single point of control for managing the entire lifecycle of an SAP system, which simplifies system management.

5. **Integration with Other SAP Modules:** SAP Solution Manager integrates with other SAP modules, such as SAP Financial Accounting (FI) and SAP Sales and Distribution (SD), to provide a complete view of the business processes.

## Conclusion:

SAP Solution Manager is a powerful tool for managing the entire lifecycle of an SAP system.

By using the system monitoring, change request management, test management, incident management, and technical monitoring features of SAP Solution Manager, businesses can efficiently manage the SAP system and improve system stability and availability.

SAP Solution Manager provides various benefits, such as improved system stability, increased efficiency, faster issue resolution, simplified system management, and integration with other SAP modules.

# 14

—Ⅲ—

## Advanced SAP System Configuration

Advanced SAP System Configuration is an advanced level of system configuration in the SAP system. It is responsible for managing the advanced features of the SAP system, which includes performance tuning, advanced security, high availability, and disaster recovery. In this chapter, we will provide an overview of Advanced SAP System Configuration, its features, and its benefits.

## Features of Advanced SAP System Configuration:

Advanced SAP System Configuration provides various features to manage the advanced features of the SAP system. Some of the key features of Advanced SAP System Configuration include:

1. **Performance Tuning:** The performance tuning feature of Advanced SAP System Configuration is used to optimize the performance of the SAP system. It enables the business to improve system response times and reduce system downtime.

2. **Advanced Security:** The advanced security feature of Advanced SAP System Configuration is used to manage the advanced security features of the SAP system, such as encryption, secure network communication, and advanced access control. It enables the business to protect sensitive data and comply with regulatory requirements.

3. **High Availability:** The high availability feature of Advanced SAP System Configuration is used to ensure that the SAP system is always available, even in the event of a system failure. It enables the business to avoid system downtime and maintain business continuity.

4. **Disaster Recovery:** The disaster recovery feature of Advanced SAP System Configuration is used to recover the SAP system in the event of a disaster. It enables the business to minimize data loss and reduce system downtime.

5. **Advanced Configuration Management:** The advanced configuration management feature of Advanced SAP System Configuration is used to manage the advanced configuration

of the SAP system, such as advanced database configuration, advanced network configuration, and advanced hardware configuration.

## Benefits of Advanced SAP System Configuration:

Advanced SAP System Configuration provides various benefits to a business. Some of the key benefits of Advanced SAP System Configuration include:

1. **Improved System Performance:** Advanced SAP System Configuration optimizes the performance of the SAP system, which enables the business to improve system response times and reduce system downtime.

2. **Increased System Security:** Advanced SAP System Configuration manages the advanced security features of the SAP system, which enables the business to protect sensitive data and comply with regulatory requirements.

3. **Enhanced Business Continuity:** Advanced SAP System Configuration ensures that the SAP system is always available, even in the event of a system failure, which enables the business to maintain business continuity.

4. **Minimized Data Loss:** Advanced SAP System Configuration enables the business to minimize data loss in the event of a disaster, which reduces the impact of system downtime on the business.

5. **Improved Configuration Management:** Advanced SAP System Configuration enables the business to manage the

advanced configuration of the SAP system more efficiently, which reduces the risk of system downtime due to configuration errors.

## Conclusion:

Advanced SAP System Configuration is an advanced level of system configuration in the SAP system.

By using the performance tuning, advanced security, high availability, disaster recovery, and advanced configuration management features of Advanced SAP System Configuration, businesses can efficiently manage the advanced features of the SAP system and improve system performance, security, business continuity, and configuration management.

Advanced SAP System Configuration provides various benefits, such as improved system performance, increased system security, enhanced business continuity, minimized data loss, and improved configuration management.

# 15

## SAP Integration and Customization

S AP Integration and Customization is a critical component of the SAP system. It is responsible for integrating the SAP system with other software systems and customizing the SAP system to meet the unique needs of a business.

In this chapter, we will provide an overview of SAP Integration and Customization, its features, and its benefits.

## Features of SAP Integration and Customization:

SAP Integration and Customization provides various features to help integrate the SAP system with other software systems and customize the SAP system. Some of the key features of SAP Integration and Customization include:

1. **Integration with Other Software Systems:** The integration feature of SAP Integration and Customization is used to integrate the SAP system with other software systems, such as customer relationship management (CRM) systems and supply chain management (SCM) systems. It enables the business to streamline business processes and improve productivity.

2. **Customization of SAP System:** The customization feature of SAP Integration and Customization is used to customize the SAP system to meet the unique needs of a business. It enables the business to configure the SAP system to support specific business processes and improve efficiency.

3. **Data Migration:** The data migration feature of SAP Integration and Customization is used to migrate data from other software systems to the SAP system. It enables the business to consolidate data and improve data accuracy.

4. **Web Services:** The web services feature of SAP Integration and Customization is used to provide access to SAP system functionality via web services. It enables the business to integrate the SAP system with other software systems that support web services.

5. **Reporting and Analytics:** The reporting and analytics feature of SAP Integration and Customization is used to create custom reports and analytics to meet the unique needs of a business. It enables the business to gain insights into business performance and make informed decisions.

## Benefits of SAP Integration and Customization:

SAP Integration and Customization provides various benefits to a business. Some of the key benefits of SAP Integration and Customization include:

1. **Streamlined Business Processes**: SAP Integration and Customization enables the business to integrate the SAP system with other software systems and streamline business processes. It improves productivity and efficiency.

2. **Customized SAP System:** SAP Integration and Customization enables the business to customize the SAP system to meet the unique needs of a business. It enables the business to configure the SAP system to support specific business processes and improve efficiency.

3. Customization enables the business to consolidate data and improve data accuracy. It enables the business to make informed decisions based on accurate data.

4. **Improved Integration with Other Software Systems:** SAP Integration and Customization enables the business to integrate the SAP system with other software systems that support web services. It enables the business to streamline business processes and improve productivity.

5. **Improved Business Intelligence:** SAP Integration and Customization enables the business to create custom reports and analytics to meet the unique needs of a business. It enables the business to gain insights into business performance and make informed decisions.

## Conclusion:

SAP Integration and Customization is a critical component of the SAP system.

By using the integration, customization, data migration, web services, and reporting and analytics features of SAP Integration and Customization, businesses can efficiently integrate the SAP system with other software systems and customize the SAP system to meet the unique needs of a business.

SAP Integration and Customization provides various benefits, such as streamlined business processes, customized SAP system, improved data accuracy, improved integration with other software systems, and improved business intelligence.

# Conclusion

— ⚍ —

In this book, we provided an overview of SAP software and its various modules, along with advanced system configuration, integration, and customization. We covered a range of topics, from basic system configuration to advanced topics like high availability and disaster recovery. We also discussed how SAP modules like FI, SD, MM, PP, HCM, and BI can help businesses manage their finances, sales, distribution, materials management, production planning, human capital management, and business intelligence.

We also discussed the importance of SAP system monitoring, change request management, test management, incident management, technical monitoring, and security and authorizations. By using these features, businesses can efficiently manage the SAP system and improve system stability, availability, and security.

In addition, we covered SAP Solution Manager, which is a centralized application management and support solution for SAP software. It provides various features to help manage the entire lifecycle of an SAP system, from implementation to maintenance.

Finally, we discussed Advanced SAP System Configuration, which is responsible for managing the advanced features of the SAP system, such as performance tuning, advanced security, high availability, and disaster recovery. By using the performance tuning, advanced security, high availability, disaster recovery, and advanced configuration management features of Advanced SAP System Configuration, businesses can efficiently manage the advanced features of the SAP system and improve system performance, security, business continuity, and configuration management.

Overall, this book provided a comprehensive overview of SAP software and its various modules, along with advanced system configuration, integration, and customization. By understanding these concepts, businesses can efficiently manage the SAP system and improve their operations. We hope this book has been informative and helpful for businesses looking to improve their SAP system management.

Printed in Great Britain
by Amazon

45052744R00050